I can't find you, Mum!

First published in this edition in 2010 by Evans Brothers Ltd
2A Portman Mansions
Chiltern Street
London W1U 6NR

Originally published in Belgium as Waar is mama?

British Library Cataloguing in Publication Data

Bode, Ann de.
   I can't find you, mum. -- (Side by side)
   1. Missing children--Juvenile fiction. 2. Hide-and-seek--
Juvenile fiction. 3. Department stores--Juvenile fiction.
   4. Mother and child--Juvenile fiction. 5. Children's stories.
   I. Title II. Series
   839.3'1364-dc22

ISBN-13: 9780237543075

Printed in China

Jessie and her mum were shopping.
Jessie was getting tired.
'Let's have a quick look at some books,'
said Mum.

Jessie found a story to read.
But before she could finish it,
Mum came to find her.

'Can we go now?' asked Jessie.
'Just one more thing,' said Mum.

Jessie sighed and followed her mum.
There were clothes everywhere.
Boring, she thought.

She hid under a rail of sweaters
and span it round and round.
'This is much more fun!' she laughed.

Jessie got tired of her game,
and crawled out.
Where's Mum? she wondered.

8

Was she trying something on?
Those are Mum's shoes! she thought.

9

Jessie swished back the curtain.
Oops! That wasn't Mum!
Jessie began to feel scared.

She looked everywhere. She raced
up and down the escalators.
No Mum.

Jessie ran to all the exits. No Mum.
Now she felt really worried.

She bumped into people and
knocked things flying.
'Hey!' someone shouted.
'Look where you're going!'
Jessie kept running. She had lost her mum.

Jessie was tired, and she
was very upset.
'I can't find you, Mum!' she cried.

Suddenly, she felt a hand on her shoulder.
Mum! she thought. But it was a
man she didn't know.
'What's the matter, little girl?' he asked.

Jessie remembered what her
mum and dad had told her:
'Don't talk to strangers, even if
they are kind.'
So she ran all the way out of the shop...

...and into the street.
The man mustn't catch up with her!

Jessie stopped at last.
Where am I? she thought.
And where's Mum?

Suddenly, across the road,
Jessie saw a policeman.
She shouted and waved.

'Help, Mr Policeman, help!' she shouted.
'I've lost my mum!'

'I'm not a policeman, I'm a
security guard,' the man said.
'But I'll find your mum for you.'

2

He took Jessie into his office.
'These nice ladies will look after you
while we find your mum,' said the
security guard.

'Let's get you something to drink,'
said one of the ladies, smiling.
'I bet you're thirsty.'
Jessie nodded.

Jessie told the nice lady about losing Mum, and the man who had frightened her.

24

The other lady came in, holding
a big teddy bear.
'This is Mr Brown,' she said. 'He's our
lucky bear. Can he sit with you?'

'How will you find Mum?' Jessie asked. 'We'll ring the shops and they'll tell their customers that you're here,' the lady said.

So Jessie waited for Mum.
She watched a funny cartoon
with Mr Brown.
She didn't notice when someone
came into the room.

'So!' said Mum. 'This is where you've been hiding – eating biscuits and watching TV!' 'Mum!' shouted Jessie. They hugged each other tight.

The nice lady came over.
'So,' she said. 'Back together,
safe and sound.'
'Yes,' agreed Mum. 'But I've never
felt so scared.'

'Next time you go shopping, you could agree where to meet in case you lose each other,' she said.
I'm not losing Mum again! thought Jessie.

It was time to go home. Jessie and her mum said thank you to everyone and waved goodbye.

Jessie stopped. 'I nearly forgot to give Mr Brown back. He *was* lucky!' she said, and kissed him on the nose.